SAVANNAH

SECRET & PUBLIC GARDENS

Photography by N. Jane Iseley · Text by James A.D. Cox

Published by Historic Savannah Foundation

Savannah, Georgia

This book is dedicated to Mary Helen Ray, whose love and enthusiasm for Savannah and
its gardens, trees, and landscapes have inspired a whole new generation of gardeners. May this book of beautiful places
remind us all of Mary Helen Ray's tireless service to our nation, state, and city through her substantial contributions
to many organizations, including the Savannah Park and Tree Commission, the Savannah Area Council of Garden Clubs,
the Savannah Tree Foundation, the Georgia Botanical Garden, and Historic Savannah Foundation.

©2000 by Historic Savannah Foundation

Graham P. Sadler, President

Mark C. McDonald, Executive Director

Photographs © 2000 by N. Jane Iseley

Text © 2000 by James A.D. Cox

Design: Palmetto Graphic Design Company

Editor: Sheryl Krieger Miller

Photography Coordinator & Stylist: Alice Turner Michalak

Special thanks to Ronald Carl Melander

Library of Congress Catalog Card Number: 00-134204
ISBN 0-9610106-2-2

Printed in Altona, Manitoba, Canada by Friesens Corp.

Columbia Square

AVANNAH! The very name brings to mind warm hospitality. From beautiful homes near the river to elegant townhouses on oak-lined avenues and spacious squares, its beauty and charm are the result of persistent efforts of a long line of dedicated individuals and groups.

The social philosophy that permeated Savannah's founding, its plan, and its early laws grew from a desire to produce healthful urban living and an equal right to property. The Savannah plan became the prototype of the earliest colonial Georgia towns. As Edmund N. Bacon stated, "It is amazing that a colony, struggling against the most elemental problems of survival in a wilderness, should be able to produce a plan so exalted that it remains as one of the finest diagrams for city organization and growth in existence."

The Trustees of the colony of Georgia in America included the Duke of Richmond, the Earl of Derby, Sir Hans Sloane, Charles DuBois, George Heathcote, James Oglethorpe, and certain members of The Worshipful Society of Apothecaries of London. Because they wanted the colony to become economically independent, they set aside a 10-acre area east of town as an experimental garden, the first technical and scientific botanical garden in America. Trustees' Garden was located on Savannah's high bluff and included a slope leading down to a small section of marsh for testing tropical or bog plants. The purpose was twofold: to serve primarily as an experimental station and as a nursery. The nursery would supply imported grapevines for the production of wine, and white mulberry trees would provide food for silkworms, which, in turn, would produce silk. It was hoped that these two industries would reduce England's trade dependence on Italy, France, and Spain.

The base crops seemed relatively successful in the beginning. Joseph Fitzwalter, Georgia's first official gardener, reported to the Trustees that the settlement had 8,000 mulberry trees to host silkworms. Unfortunately, it soon became clear that the climate was not ideal for cultivation of the trees. Other plants from various countries were introduced to the gardens. These included apples, plums, pears, figs, pomegranates, oranges, tea (which proved to be too expensive), bamboo from the East Indies, olives, peaches, alfalfa, and various herbs.

Two significant botanists who spearheaded the colony's earliest plant collections were Dr. William Houston and Philip Miller. Miller was the Society of Apothecaries' gardener in charge of the famous Chelsea Physic Garden in London. Among the species he sent were seeds of *catharantus roseus*, the Madagascar Periwinkle (a valuable plant in cancer research), and, it is said, the seeds of Upland Cotton. That cottonseed, a minor item at the time, became the important parent of cotton in the United States. From it, the greater part of the world's cotton is descended.

Spanish Moss and Azaleas in Forsyth Park

In 1738, a spring freeze was followed by a summer drought, which wrought havoc with the newly introduced plants. The garden was designed by trained horticulturists in England, however, expert guidance was often missing on the garden site itself.

Although the Trustees' Garden lasted only 22 years, it was a brave experiment. It tested foods and plants and proved which were of value to the colony and which were not. The Chelsea Physic Garden botanists encouraged the cultivation of herbs in this garden. On June 12, 1983, the American Institute of Pharmacy, in cooperation with the Georgia Pharmaceutical Association, recognized the importance of the Trustees' Garden. The dedication of a bronze marker on the original site was made to commemorate the 250th anniversary of the founding of the Trustees' Garden. Dr. Douglas Whittet, Master of that same Worshipful Society of Apothecaries of London that had provided the first consignment of seeds, was invited as principal speaker for the occasion. Another distinguished guest was Max Cleland, U.S. Senator from Georgia and a graduate pharmacist. Botanical historians consider the Trustees' Garden to be in the same category as Monticello, Mount Vernon, and Bartram's Garden.

Early in Savannah's history the city was called "The Forest City." In 1896, the Georgia General Assembly and Savannah's mayor and aldermen passed legislation to create a five-member Park and Tree Commission. The Commission protected the trees and parks of Savannah, recommended programs to enhance and add to its beauty, guided and educated the public about the value and benefits of trees to this community, and sought assistance from the public to protect trees from disease, pollution, and unnecessary destruction. The dedication displayed by this Commission followed faithfully the path set by James Oglethorpe, Savannah's founder.

The first Park and Tree Commission in 1896 announced to its citizens, "We believe that the magnificent Live Oak (*Quercus virginiana*) and the picturesque Palmetto to be the distinct characteristic feature of our flora and should appear in every point of vantage."

The surge of citizen pride and concern for Savannah's trees was exemplified in a new and improved Land Clearing and Tree Protection Ordinance (1995), which promises to guide development of future community health and growth of trees. Among an increasing number of citizen, neighborhood and community tree programs are those of the Savannah Tree Foundation, the Chatham County Community Tree Program, the City of Savannah Master Reforestation Plan, and Historic Savannah Foundation's Landmark District Tree Fund.

Led by Citizens Forestry Support System in 1994, a Savannah Urban Forest Summit meeting was held to improve the communication and efficiency of Savannah's urban forest management. The Summit consisted of representatives of City Council, Park and Tree Commission members, the Park and Tree Department, the City staff, the Savannah Tree Foundation, the Chatham County Tree Commission, and the Chatham County School Administration. The Park and Tree Commission was expanded from five to nine members with each member corresponding to a City Council position including the size of aldermanic districts. This broadened community representation. General Oglethorpe's principles of representation were continued.

The Park and Tree Commission has enjoyed extensive cooperation from the garden clubs of Savannah in their contributions toward beautification of the historic district. Leading the effort is the Trustees Garden Club. According to the club records, "In 1957, the Park and Tree Commission asked the Club to improve the 14-block length of Emmett Park (on the bluff overlooking the river), which at that time was unplanted and being considered for a parking lot. Along with the addition of plants, shrubs and grass, the Club installed brick walks, a length of antique iron fencing and 13,950 bulbs. Local businessmen, impressed by the Club's work (in their 10-year project) and led by the Chamber of Commerce, formed a Bay Street Merchants Association which pledge yearly subscriptions to help the Club in its care of the park."

Other civic projects of the Trustees Garden Club included extensive restoration in 1967–1970 of Colonial Park Cemetery (1750–1853) and restoration in 1970 of Columbia Square (laid out in 1799). This latter project concluded with the installation of a memorial fountain in 1972 and colorful annuals in 1977.

Other garden clubs have contributed annually to beautification of the historic district, including the Downtown Garden Club and the Garden Club of Savannah (which sponsors the annual NOGS Tour of gardens located north of Gaston Street). There is also the Chatham County Council of Garden Clubs. Our citizen gardeners and garden clubs continue to encourage visitors and tours to enjoy the classic beauty inspired by General Oglethorpe's vision of 1733 with the seeds sown in Savannah's Trustees' Garden.

The Park and Tree Commission invites contributions for the planting of trees in public areas. Individuals, corporations, or other groups can make tax-deductible contributions to the Tribute Tree Fund, or the Landmark District Tree Fund, to honor a person or special event.

In her deep concern over the "Vanishing Gardens of Savannah," Laura Palmer Bell in 1944 asked landscape architect Clermont Lee to make carefully measured drawings of the few remaining gardens in Savannah. Bell later reported, "While there were ever fewer than I thought, her scale drawings show how charming are the patterns of the gardens that were laid out so many years ago, and that the few that are now well kept are evidence of how lovely the town must have been when all were planted."

Lee was asked by the Girl Scouts of the USA to design a garden for their national headquarters, the Wayne Gordon House on Oglethorpe Avenue. Lee produced a period parterre design (circa 1860–1886), which continues to enhance the visitor's experience of the birthplace of Juliette Gordon Low.

In the more than 265 years since the founding of this unique colony with an early experimental public garden, there have been many alterations to Savannah's urban fabric. However, Oglethorpe's and the Trustees' original conception of Savannah remained a strong guiding principle for the numerous individuals and groups who have played major roles in shaping Savannah's history as a garden city. ❧

– Mary Helen Ray

"The Air is healthy, being always serene, pleasant and temperate, never subject to excessive Heat or Cold,

nor to sudden Changes; the Winter is regular and short, and Summer cool'd with refreshing Breezes. The Soil of this Country is

generally Sandy, especially near the Sea; but 'tis impregnated with such a fertile mixture that they use no Manure, even in their most

ancient Settlements, which have been under tillage these sixty years. It will produce almost every

Thing in wonderful quantities with very little Culture."

SUCH WAS THE ENCOURAGING PROMISE GIVEN IN *A New and Accurate Account of the Provinces of South Carolina and Georgia* printed in London in 1732 to persuade prospective colonists to consider passage to this new colony.

Prior to the founding of Savannah, two voyagers — a naturalist and a botanist — traveled extensively in Carolina (including the land to become Georgia). A young Englishman named John Lawson arrived in Carolina in 1700 and spent the next eight years exploring and hunting for plants, which led to the publication in London in 1709 of *A New Voyage to Carolina, containing the Exact Description and Natural History of the Country, together with the Present State Therof, and a Journal of a Thousand Miles Travel'd thro' Several Nations of Indians. Giving a particular Account of their Customs, manners, etc.* In addition to his extensive and detailed lists of trees, vegetables, fruit, herbs, plants, and shrubs, he wrote, "The Flower-Garden in Carolina is as yet arrived, but to a very poor and jejune perfection. We have only two sorts of Roses; the Clove-July-Flowers, Violets, Princes Feather and Tres colors. There has been nothing more cultivated in the Flower-Garden, which at present, occurs to my memory; but for the wild spontaneous Flowers of the Country, Nature has been so liberal that I cannot name one tenth part of the valuable ones." To titillate the imaginations and appetites of avid plant collectors, he adds, "And at present the curious may have a large field to satisfy and divert themselves in, as collections of strange Beasts, Birds, Insects, Reptiles, Shells, Fishes, Minerals, Herbs, Flowers, Plants, Shrubs, Intricate Roots, Gums, Tears, Rosins, Dyes and Stones."

Mark Catesby must have been familiar with Lawson's book when he arrived in Charleston in 1722. He had previously spent five years in Virginia collecting seeds, plants, and specimens to send back to horticulturists in England and making exquisite drawings of flora and fauna. During the years he spent in Carolina and Florida, including a long spell at Fort Moore on the upper reaches of the Savannah River, he directed his attention to plants and also focused on birds, both of which are frequently featured together in his illustrations. The first volume of The Natural History of Carolina, Florida and the Bahama Islands was published in 1731.

The County of Savannah illustrating town, garden, and farm lots (c. 1740).

Both Lawson and Catesby received assistance from friendly Indians. Indeed, in spite of the Yamasee War of 1715–1716, Carolinians had made strong bonds with Indians on their borders, especially in the land between the Savannah and the Altamaha rivers, where boundaries had never been satisfactorily defined. In 1717, Sir Robert Mountgomery, a Scottish baronet, proposed to found a colony there to be called the Margravate of Azilia and devised an elaborate but strictly geometric plan for it. For lack of adequate funding, the scheme failed. A Swiss merchant, Jean Pierce Purry, proposed a more modest settlement that eventually came to fruition in 1730 on the north side of the Savannah River. It was named Purrysburg.

A proprietorship since 1663, South Carolina became a Royal Colony in 1729, and the British government took more seriously the need for defense, but this was not the main concern of a proposal put forward in 1730 by James Edward Oglethorpe. As chairman of a parliamentary committee to inquire into "the State of the Gaols of the Kingdom," he became aware of the plight of the unemployed and of those who had sunken into indebtedness. Together with his fellow committeeman, Sir John Percival (created first Earl of Egmont in 1733), and other trustees, he launched a proposal for the establishment of the colony of Georgia in America. In addition to providing able-bodied armed men to aid in defense, the colony was to produce silk, wine and spices that otherwise had to be imported to England at great expense from Europe and the East. The charter received the royal assent on April 21, and the 114 selected colonists sailed on the "Anne" from Gravesend on November 17, 1732, accompanied by Oglethorpe. It took almost two months to reach Charleston and, after a brief sojourn at Port Royal, the party landed at Yamacraw Bluff on February 12, 1733. They were fortunate to find a friendly Indian village, led by King Tomochichi, and the trading post of John Musgrove, whose wife, Mary, became Oglethorpe's interpreter. With considerable assistance from the Governor and Assembly of South Carolina, both with supplies and manpower, work progressed surprisingly quickly in developing the town.

There has been considerable scholarly speculation about the genesis of the Savannah town plan. Certainly it had been formulated in London and approved by the Trustees before the "Anne" sailed. Classical Roman colonial planning, building for military defense, contemporary town planning in Ireland, freemasonry, and even current kitchen garden design have all been explored, but in his essay in *Forty Years of Diversity — Essays on Colonial Georgia*, John W. Reps has made the strongest case for the familiarity shared by most of the Trustees with the newly laid out London squares.

The scheme is disarmingly simple: the creation of an open square entered centrally north and south, with east-west crossroads at each end and in the center. This creates 10 building lots measuring 60 by 90 feet north and south and four larger trust lots for public buildings. Allowing for this pattern to be repeated as much as required, there was a commons to the south beyond which were gardens embracing five acres and then larger square farms amounting to 44 acres and 140 poles. Each male adult was granted a lot, a garden, and a farm — 50 acres in all. He was required to plant 100 white mulberry trees and to fence his holdings to prevent them from "the bite of cattle." In addition, he had to agree to remain in the colony for at least three years and to spend the first year laboring at public works. The Trustees forbade the sale of rum or the introduction of slaves.

After only a month, the South Carolina Gazette reported on March 22, "There are no idlers here. He [Oglethorpe] has plowed up some Land part of which is sowed with Wheat which is come up and looks promising. He has two or three Gardens which he has sowed with diverse Sorts and Seeds and planted Thyme with other sorts of Potherbs, Sage, Leeks, Skallions, Celeri, Liquorice Etc. and several sorts of Fruit trees." In addition, 10 acres of land to the east of the town formed a Trustees' Garden, to serve as a nursery and for the propagation of white mulberry trees used as food for silk worms.

The houses were simple: one story, with attic space, measuring 24 by 16 feet placed centrally on the front of the 60-foot-wide lot, leaving plenty of space around it, which was fenced. This space was used for domestic purposes such as hanging out clothes to dry, domesticated animals, and for raising foodstuffs. In 1745, *London Magazine* reported, "The Houses are built some distance from each other, to allow more Air and Garden Room, and prevent the Communication, in Case of Accident by Fire. … They have a publick garden, in a very thriving Way, which is a Kind of Nursery for the Use of the Inhabitants. The Town stands about ten Miles from the Sea up the River, (which is navigable some hundred Miles from the Country,) and is, certainly a very good Harbour, and well seated for Trade. The land, a considerable Space round the Town, is well clear'd, and the Passages lie open: a handsome Road-Way running above a Mile from it, and making the Prospect very lightsome." For the first 50 years, the town consisted of six squares. Ellis Square was the market, where vegetables from the farms, together with meat and fish, were sold.

In 1750, after the ban on slavery was lifted by the Trustees, some prosperity came to Savannah. A large number of Savannahians owned plantations and summer homes, and the development of the port increased contacts with the outside world. One successful merchant was James Habersham, who had served as superintendent of the orphanage founded in 1740 by the Reverend George Whitefield at Bethesda, 10 miles south of Savannah. Habersham built up a mercantile shipping company that traded with firms in London. Recognizing that the growing of mulberry trees and vineyards had not been successful, Habersham turned to rice with great success. Soon he owned 198 slaves, and his plantation, Silk Hope, grew to 100,000 acres. The great plantations or country seats of the wealthy colonists became the sites of the first pleasure gardens of Georgia.

To obtain seeds and plants, gardeners had to look north beyond the Savannah River. In Philadelphia, John Bartram had established the first botanic garden in America in 1730. In order to satisfy the requirements of English collectors, Bartram was commissioned to search for more specimens. Indeed, plants from seeds he sent to London were drawn by Mark Catesby for later volumes of his book. One of few native-born Americans of his time to search for plants, Bartram was equally interested in plant physiology, rocks and minerals, birds, insects, and animals. His travels took him from upper New York to Florida, latterly accompanied by his son,

William. When in Georgia they discovered the rare white flowered *Franklinia alatamaha*, which was last seen growing in the wild in 1803. Originally named *Gordonia pubescens*, the name was changed in 1785 to honor Benjamin Franklin. William returned to collect seeds of it several years later, too late for his father to see it bloom. William published his *Travels through North and South Carolina, Georgia, East and West Florida* in 1791. He writes of his last visit to Georgia: "Left Savanna [sic] in the evening, in consequence of a pressing invitation from the honorable Jonathan Bryan, Esq. who was returning from the capital, to his villa, about eight miles up Savanna river; a very delightful situation, where are spacious gardens, furnished with variety of fruit trees and flowering shrubs; observed on a low wet place at the corner of the garden, the Ado (*Arum esculentum*) this plant is much cultivated in the maritime parts of Georgia and Florida for the sake of its large Turnip-like root, which when boiled or roasted, is excellent food, and tastes like the Yam; the leaves of this magnificent plant are very large and circulated, the spadix

*J*ohn Abbot's *Erythrina herbacea*

———

terminates with a very long subulated tongue, naked and perfectly white; perhaps this may be the Arum Colocasia."

John Abbot, Englishman, artist, and naturalist, spent 64 years in residence in Georgia beginning in 1776. He achieved renown among European and American naturalists for his life's work in the study of natural history in the area of the lush Savannah River Valley. In *John Abbot in Georgia: The Vision of a Naturalist Artist*, Vivian Rogers-Price writes, "Fewer than 200 of his watercolors were published, a mere fraction of the more than 5,000 that he completed in his lifetime. His discoveries rank alongside those of William Bartram (1739–1823), Alexander Wilson (1766–1813), and John James Audubon (1785–1851)."

Savannah's aspiring gardeners had access to numerous nurseries in South Carolina. Henry Laurens and Dr. Alexander Garden both had town gardens in Charleston and countryseats not too far away. John Bartram visited Laurens' town garden in 1765 and noted it walled with brick, 200 yards long and 150 yards wide. It was "enriched with everything useful and ornamental that Carolina produced or his mercantile connections enabled him to procure from remote parts of the world. Among a variety of other curious productions, he introduced olives, capers, limes, ginger, guinea grass, the alpine strawberry, bearing nine months of the year, red raspberrys, blue grapes; and also directly from the south of France, apples, pears, and plumbs of fine kinds, and vines which bore abundantly of the choice white eating grape called Chasselates blancs." Dr. Garden's competence as a botanist was widely recognized throughout the southern colonies and in England: The cape jasmine was named Gardenia jasminoides for him.

Robert Squibb was born in England and came to Charleston in 1780. He immediately became a citizen and opened a nursery on Tradd Street. Because there was a lack of information about the cultivation of garden plants in the New World and English garden books were not written with Carolina or Georgia climate and soils in mind, he wrote and had published in 1787 *The Gardeners Callender for South Carolina, Georgia and North Carolina*, believing that climate and topography were similar in all these states. It is a practical monthly guide to garden duties. By the time of his death in 1806, he was superintendent of the botanical gardens at Silk Hope, the Habersham plantation near Savannah.

André Michaux, botanist to Loius XVI of France, spent 11 years between 1785 and 1796 collecting plants in the eastern States. He was a frequent visitor to John Bartram's garden. Having established a nursery in New Jersey, he purchased 200 acres on the Ashley River outside Charleston, which became his home. In addition to sending specimens to France, Michaux imported seeds of trees that were to have considerable impact on Southern streets and gardens: the crepe myrtle (*Lagerstromia indica*), the mimosa (*Albisia julibrissin*), as well as pomegranates (*Punica Granatum*), the Japanese camellia (*Camellia japonica*), and Azalea indica (*Rhododendron luteum*). Michaux may also have introduced the Maidenhair tree (*Gingko biloba*) and the Chinaberry (*Melia azedarach*).

In 1792 a disastrous fire swept through Savannah, devastating the area between Bay and Broughton streets and destroying some 229 structures, mostly built of wood. However, this disaster did not hamper growing prosperity, largely brought about by Eli Whitney's invention of the cotton gin at Mulberry Grove Plantation near Savannah. More squares were laid out between 1790 and 1815, and port facilities were expanded to cope with the cotton trade. In 1810, Robert Mackay, a local merchant, wrote to his wife, "The improvements are very great, Bolton is beautifying the Bay with ranges of most elegant and extensive warehouses — Commerce row is pulled down and a superb edifice with a Steeple as high almost as the Exchange has suddenly been rear'd in its place — every square in town is now enclosed with light cedar posts painted white and a chain along their tops, trees planted within, and two paved paths across, the remainder of the ground they are spreading Bermuda grass over, and upon the whole the Town looks quite another thing and very enchanting."

By the early 1820s, the houses being built were more substantial both in accommodation and construction. A house like the brick one built by Isaiah Davenport in 1820 on the corner of Habersham and East State streets is built up to the street line of Columbia Square, whereas those on a trust lot have the building set back from the road, allowing for a small amount of planting in front. Between house and carriage house, there was a courtyard that was utilitarian but would have had a flower garden. The young English architect William Jay built a handful of houses in the city between 1817 and 1820, including the Richardson (Owens-Thomas), Scarbrough, and Telfair houses. Unfortunately, none of the original gardens still exist, but two have been created in the later part of the 20th century.

An Englishman from Liverpool who made a number of visits to the town in the early 1820s recorded the observations, "The Streets are unpaved and except in the middle path, which is heavy disagreeable sand, they are covered with grass … its streets are planted so thick with the pride of China that the small dark houses are hardly seen … the gardens are filled with flowers, especially with a variety of roses … picturesque houses standing at intervals with rich gardens between. It's whole plan and arrangement fit it for the climate. The broad regular streets are lined with luxuriant melia and locust trees."

Early engraving of JohnsonSquare c.1844

For the keen gardener, there were only a few American gardening books available at Colonel Williams' bookshop on Bay Street, where the small private reading room upstairs held newspapers and journals from all over. *The American Gardeners Calendar* by Bernard McMahon had appeared in 1806, but then, in 1841, Andrew Jackson Downing published his *Landscape Gardening: A treatise on the theory and practice of landscape gardening adjusted to America with a view to the improvement of country residences*. In it he said very little about how to garden, though he did awaken Americans to an awareness that gardens should have an artistic "wholeness," and to recognize their picturesque native landscape. Stephen Elliot read and studied it.

Known as Georgia's Planting Prelate, Elliot was consecrated first Episcopal Bishop of Georgia in the newly rebuilt Christ Church in 1841, a position he held for 25 years until his death in 1866. In addition to being a keen and learned gardener, he established

The broad regular streets are lined with melia and locust trees.

————

15 new churches in the state, created a church school for boys and girls at Montpellier (which he ran for a while), and, together with Bishop James Hervey of Tennessee and Bishop Leonides Polk of Louisiana, was a founder of the University of the South at Sewanee, Tennessee. Although he was born in Beaufort, South Carolina, he considered himself a Savannahian because his mother was a Habersham.

Such was Bishop Elliot's standing in the horticultural world that he was invited to give the address before the Southern Central Agricultural Society's meeting in Macon in 1851. He opened by saying, "It seems at first sight very astonishing that in a state blessed as Georgia with all the advantages of nature, so little attention should have been paid to Horticulture, either as a science or an art." He listed what he considered the three reasons for this: the very bounty of nature leads to a lack of enterprise; as the state grew west-wards, the frontier towns had little time for finesse; and there was a lack of horticulture books. "Why, even to this day, we have not a decent work upon the very commonest topics of vegetable or floral cultivation adapted to the South." (Robert Squibbs' book must have been long out of print.)

The bulk of this address was devoted to the cultivation of fruit trees in particular and a large range of southern vegetables. He urged his audience to export their produce and flowers. "We can place vegetables upon the northern tables perfectly matured, before their climate will permit them to be even planted … if you could witness the surprise of the northern invalids who resort to Savannah and the eastern shores of Georgia and Florida at the profusion of exquisite flowers that are poured upon them, in mid-winter from the gardens of its citizens, you would appreciate the advantages which we possess in climate and soil."

Bishop Elliot lived to see the culmination of the building of Savannah's squares in 1856 and the creation of Forsyth Park. This park was the brainchild of William B. Hodgson and was designed by Wilhelm Christian Bischoff, a Bavarian landscape architect. The effervescent cast-iron fountain was added in 1858. Thirty years later, I.W. Avery, writing in *Harper's New Monthly Magazine*, gave a fulsome description: "Forsyth Park is the most lovely spot in the city, terminating Bull Street. It contains twenty acres in the park proper, enclosed with an iron fence. It was named after one of our most brilliant Georgians, John Forsyth, United States Senator in 1818 and 1830, and Governor in 1827. This enclosure presents a unique appearance, its basic element being a forest of stately pines that contrast strikingly with the exquisite scheme of garden beneath, laid tastefully off into winding walks, grass swards, vivid groupings of bright plants and flowers, such as coleus, roses, cacti, and dahlias, and fantastic mounds of luxuriant vines. The central fountain is a gem of its kind, and leaves a living memory of poetic picturesqueness."

In 1853, the 100-year-old Colonial Cemetery, which had become engulfed by the developing city, was closed by municipal authority and became a public park. Meanwhile, a new cemetery at Laurel Grove had been established in 1845 and another at Bonaventure in 1869. These were, and still are, arboreous refuges for sauntering and family picnics.

A Park and Tree Commission was appointed after the devastation of the city's trees by a severe hurricane in 1893. These had been sugarberries, chinaberries, and sycamores that had replaced the old growth pines wiped out in an earlier hurricane in 1798. Live oaks, magnolias, and palmettos planted after 1890 grace the streets and squares today.

In a paper read before the Savannah Historical Research Association in 1940, Laura Palmer Bell recalled the gardens of her childhood in the 1880s, "There have always been flowers that refuse to be restrained by any wall, and in Savannah of fifty years ago, roses, jessamine and other vines climbed the high brick walls to look into many a quiet street, and ripe fruit and flowering shrubs were tantalizingly visible, high above the reach of envious hands. All over town at that time there were big sprawling walled gardens, flower filled back yards completely hidden from the street, a few front gardens, and many side gardens planted in orderly parterres." She rued the destruction of such gardens through the paving of the streets and the advent of the automobile.

Athens, Georgia, formed the first garden club in the United States of America in 1890, but it was not until 1926 that Trustees Garden Club was founded in Savannah. Others followed, including a men's club, particularly concerned with camellias and roses, and the Garden Club of Savannah, which organizes the annual spring NOGS Tour — gardens north of Gaston Street. Members of the Savannah Area Council of Garden Clubs also assist with the annual Tour of Homes and Gardens, which was started in 1935 by the Episcopal Women of Christ Church. Since 1976, this tour has been jointly sponsored by Historic Savannah Foundation.

Historic Savannah Foundation came into existence in 1955 largely in response to the consternation caused by the near destruction of the Davenport House and later the actual destruction of the old city market in Ellis Square. Two west-side squares had already been sacrificed for state highway improvements in the 1930s. There was a national trend for cities to sweep away the old in favor of the new, or "contemporary" as it was being termed. When houses went, so did gardens.

Historic Savannah Foundation was able to galvanize public spirit and civic awareness to the extent that Savannah could be

Forsyth Park's cast-iron fountain was added in 1858 (c.1860).

———

designated a National Historic Landmark District by the Department of the Interior in 1966. Trustees Garden Club rescued Emmett Park on the bluff above the river from becoming another parking lot in 1957. The club next undertook the restoration of Colonial Park Cemetery and in 1970 began carrying out the landscaping of Columbia Square. Of the 24 original squares, the surviving 21 and Forsyth Park were, and still are, cared for by the city's Park and Tree Department. Prompted by the renewed spirit of beautification, the city and private foundations began a major revitalization, including Bull Street and the river front plaza.

The extraordinary popularity of interest in gardening, garden design, and garden history during the last third of the 20th century coincided with the rebirth of the Savannah walled garden. Among historic homes, some 19th-century parterre layouts had survived, but for the most part it was a new beginning. Property on trust lots or with side yards had some room to play with, but because of the discipline of the city plan, most houses have very small back yards.

Some yards are truly "secret" — other than from the house, they can only be approached from the lanes that run between the streets. Here may be found cast-iron furniture, sculpture, water — and lots of pots. The seasonal changes that occur in this semi-tropical climate allow an essentially green space to turn into a blaze of color. There is an infinite variety of arrangements and choice of plantings. It is no longer necessary to travel far for specimens; they can be found at local nurseries or from catalogs and on the Internet. Savannah gardens are rich, personal, and inventive — individual Edens that encapsulate the paradise those first Georgia colonists hoped to find. ❧

James A.D. Cox

THE HOUSE WAS BUILT IN 1849 TO DESIGNS BY JOHN S. NORRIS. THE FRONT GARDEN (*below*) RETAINS THE PARTERRES much as they were originally, here aglow with a medley of pansies (*following pages*). After the death of Juliette Gordon Low in 1927, the property was acquired by the National Society of the Colonial Dames of America in the State of Georgia. The figure in the garden wall niche (*right*) was sculpted by Juliette Gordon Low. The Girl Scouts of the U.S.A. was founded in the carriage house in 1912. The courtyard paving behind the house *(pages 22–23)* was designed in the 1970s by Clermont H. Lee, noted landscape architect and native Savannahian, and is shown here with dogwood, azalea, and the white and scarlet blooms of intertwining Rosa banksiae 'Alba Plena' and honeysuckle (*Lonicera sempervirens*). ❧

A PASSERBY, ADMIRING THE WAY BIRDS FOOT ENGLISH IVY (*right*) HAS BEEN TRAINED TO HIGHLIGHT THE STONE
steps leading to the front door of the 1856 house or getting a glimpse through the adjacent wrought-iron gate, should have
no doubt that the owner is a devoted gardener. The iron balustrade was commisioned from Ivan Bailey. The design is based
on coastal birds and bull rushes and includes a heron whose raised leg acts as a convienient boot scraper. Nestled in fig
vine (*Ficus pumila*), a terra-cotta container (*below, left*) becomes a handy place for working tools. What is now the garden
(*below, right*) was a vacant space when the property was purchased by the current owner in 1973. It forms an L shape
on two sides of the house. A sunken rectangular portion has parterres in the middle edged by clipped Korean boxwood
(*Buxus microphylla 'koreana'*) and a central pool. The cast-iron fountain with a leaden figure of a boy clutching a dolphin
was made in New York by the J.W. Fiske Foundry and came to Savannah in 1870 for another garden. The millstone set
in paving came from a farm in Clarke County, Georgia, that belonged to the owner's great-grandfather.

At the axis of the L (*previous pages*), there is a circular mound of clipped native holly (*Ilex vomitoria*) with the initial letters of the four compass points formed in it. Around the perimeter are satellites of rounded holly (*Ilex vomitoria schellings dwarf*) and segmental parterres. Pink astilbe gives a splash of color. Before work was begun in 1976, the garden plan was formulated from the balcony of the carriage house. Although the design was geometric and axial, now that it is 24 years old, it is mature and romantic, even Old World. In front of a 17th-century terra-cotta Italian oil storage jar bearing the Medici arms (*left*) is a grouping of perennials, including yellow yarrow (*Achillea sp.*), larkspur (*Delphinium sp.*), white gaura lindheimeri, and pink statice (*Limonium sp.*). Fishbone fern (*Nephrolepis cordifolia*) is volunteering among liriope (*below*), pea gravel, and an adjacent stone in front of an azalea and barberry (*Berberis julianae*).

Considered the oldest town garden in Georgia, it was laid out in 1852, the same year the Barbados-style house was built. The term parterre is from a French phrase meaning "on the surface of the ground" and refers to an arrangement of beds and flowers laid out in a regular ornamental manner. It was very popular in side gardens in Savannah in the mid-19th century, influenced, no doubt, by books by John Claudius Louden and his wife, Jane, who particularly urged women to garden. It was also one of the forms recommended by Andrew Jackson Downing. These geometric patterns (*below, left; right; following pages*) were meant to be looked down upon and are particularly well suited for this long verandah and porch. The beds are bordered by molded Japanese boxwood (*Buxus microphylla 'japonica'*) and edged with ceramic tiles. They are planted with annuals and accented by tree roses. The vertical gardening seen here and along the lane gives color variety through changing seasons with a blend of wisteria, Rosa banksiae, Cherokee rose (*Rosa laevigata*), Virgin's bower (*Clematis virginiana*), and confederate jasmine (*Trachelospermum jasminoides*). A white butterfly ginger lily (*Hedychium coronarium*) blooms (*below, right*). ❦

ON THE SOUTHERN EDGE OF THE DESIGNATED HISTORIC DISTRICT, THIS LARGE GARDEN (*following pages*) is dominated by an immense old live oak (*not pictured*), one of the oldest in the Historic District — 250–300 years old. In 1992, James Morton was asked by the current owners to design garden spaces to complement the tree. Taking care not to crowd the tree, an oval of Asiatic jasmine ground cover was chosen as a protective zone under the immense live oak. Other ground covers were used as well, including mondo grass (*Liriope muscari*). Pansies and snapdragons (*below*) make a beautiful color blended border. Massed azaleas (R. 'Mrs. G.G. Gerbing' and R. 'George Tabor') are typical of a Savannah spring (*right*). ✧

THE HOUSE, DESIGNED BY WILLIAM JAY IN 1818, AND THE GARDEN ARE OPEN TO VISITORS. SET BACK FROM THE street (*right*), the house is on a trust lot overlooking Oglethorpe Square's azaleas and dogwood trees. The original formal garden was on a separate lot across State Street. After a restoration of the house in 1954, Clermont H. Lee designed a formal parterre garden behind the house in the former service yard using native plants. In 1985, an extensive refurbishing of the garden was undertaken by Louisa Farrand Wood, then Head Gardener (*following pages*). Four Russian-Olive trees (*Elaeagnus angustifolia*), which are rarely planted in Savannah, and much of the remaining plant material were removed. Today the garden is maintained by a committee of volunteers whose duties include the planting of pansies in the parterre beds in early November and begonias in early May. In the foreground are Hibiscus (*H. Rosa-sinensis*) in pots and a fig tree (*Ficus carica*). The central pool was installed in 1990 and dedicated to Mrs. Wood. Across the clipped hedges of dwarf yaupon holly (*Ilex vomitoria 'Nana'*), there is an espalier pyracantha and a rosemary bush in the herbaceous border (*below, left*). The overhanging branch is from a flowering apricot tree (*Prunus Mume*) saved from the earlier planting. The pots (*below, right*) contain agapanthus and hibiscus in front of a Cherokee rose *(Rosa laevigata)*. ❧

THIS PARTERRE GARDEN PROBABLY DATES FROM THE BUILDING OF THE HOUSE IN 1859 (*following pages*). THE UPTURNED stout bottles that form the edging of the flower beds bear the date of 1840. The present owners have converted the central oval bed into a pool surrounded by a bed of ajuga. The fountain (*below, left*) was found in an antiques shop, but it is not very old. It is Italian and bears the name Maturn Mercau. Blooming in fall and winter are yellow cassia (*below, right*) and camellias Sasanqua (*right*). ❧

THE GARDEN WAS CREATED AFTER THE HOUSE HAD BEEN REFURBISHED AND GIVEN AN ADDITION IN 1993. THE OLD FRENCH lantern over the original gate *(right; below, left)* was found in an antiques shop in Dallas, Texas, by designer Joci Firth and is supported by an iron scroll designed by Randolph Martz and cast by Greg Royer. A slate flag path with intervening dwarf mondo grass (*Ophiopogon japonicus 'Nana'*) leads through an evergreen grove that includes cone shaped Foster's holly (*Ilex x attenuata 'Fosteri'*), Japanese maple, crepe myrtle, and Chinese juniper (*Juniper chinensis var. torulosa*). A serpentine stack stone wall (*below, right*) supports a planting with a beautiful show of summer flowers. The rain lilies (*Zephyranthes grandiflora*) found their way up through a deep layer of soil. Camellia Sasanqua, liriope, English ivy, wild honeysuckle (*Lonicera sempervirens),* and red trumpet vine (*Campsis radicans)* are among the species shown. ❧

DESIGNED FOR CHARLES GREEN IN 1853 BY JOHN S. NORRIS, THIS TUDOR REVIVAL HOUSE HAS A PARTERRE garden to the east (*right*) facing Madison Square. The layout is original, but the planting scheme is modern. The house was purchased by St. John's Church in 1943 to be used as a parish house, and in 1960, the city allowed the closure of Macon Street, which ran between the two buildings. A median garden (*below*) was designed by Clermont H. Lee with a central pool containing a fountain in the form of a fish sculpted by Maclean Marshall of Rome, Georgia. ❧

EVERYTHING IN THIS LUSH GARDEN RESTS UPON A SOLID CONCRETE BASE, WHICH HAD BEEN USED AS A CAR PARK when the property was purchased in 1978 (*right*). The cast-iron urn is dated April 2, 1879 — the year before the house was built. The aedicule between a pair of sphinxes (*below*) houses a painted cast dolphin spouting onto a terra-cotta slab saved from the Odd Fellows Building that was torn down. Designed to be looked down upon, the pond (*following pages*) is backed by four sago palms (*Cycas revoluta*) and a pair of English terra-cotta urns. It is full of water hyacinth (*Eichhornia crassipes*), fairy moss (*Azolla caroliniana*), water lettuce (*Pistia stratiotes*), and a stand of umbrella grass (*Cyperus alternifolius*). ❧

THIS PROPERTY WAS PURCHASED IN 1953 BY THE GIRL SCOUTS OF THE USA AS A MEMORIAL TO their founder who was born in this house in 1860. There is no evidence of what the former garden was like. The existing parterre layout (*below, left*) was designed by Clermont H. Lee and installed in 1956, using plants available in Savannah before 1886, including the Century plants (*Agave americana*). The 1840 Japanese cast-bronze Emperor cranes set in fatsia (*below, right*) were presented in tribute to Page Wilder Anderson, the first Girl Scout troop leader.

SEEN THROUGH A GNARLED OLD CREPE MYRTLE TREE *(below, right)*, THIS TRIM YARD IS BEHIND A PAIR OF

houses in Gordon Row. The lawn is separated by a carefully clipped Japanese holly hedge. A keen grower maintains the

pots on the balconies, which need constant watering, often twice a day in the summer. Beneath the flowering Confederate

jasmine *(Trachelospermum jasminoides)* on the balustrade *(below, left)* are healthy geraniums that may flourish year-round

in all but the hottest summer months, given enough sun and protection from the rare winter freeze.

THE TERRACE WAS DESIGNED BY JIM WILLIAMS WHEN HE RESTORED THE HOUSE IN 1960.
It is an extension of the living area, the floor of which appears to flow out to the pool (*below*) surrounded with ferns,
including holly fern (*Cyrtomium falcatum*), a variety of angel wing begonias, and aucuba (*A. japonica*) enjoying
a splash of sun. The statue and the obelisks are Italian.

THIS SIDE GARDEN (*below*) IS DOMINATED BY AN IMMENSE CREPE MYRTLE (*LAGERSTROEMIA INDICA*), PROBABLY one of the oldest specimens in America, certainly older than the house, which was built in 1853. Crepe Myrtles were introduced to the east coast of North America from Persia by André Michaux toward the end of the 18th century. Along the wall is an espaliered camellia Sasanqua, and in the foreground is a mature sago palm (*Cycas revoluta*). ❧

BY 1991, THIS COTTAGE, WHICH HAD BEEN DERELICT FOR SOME TIME, HAD BEEN FULLY RESTORED. THE EAST

facing garden (*right*) designed by Cynthia White has crepe myrtle 'Natchez' and Foster's Holly (*Ilex x attenuata*), a hedge of

Pittosporum Tobira, together with fencing and a brick terrace. The owner is an avid plant collector and has devised a virtual outdoor

greenhouse assembling a countless variety of interesting pots. On looking down from the balcony, there is a splendid view of the

garden in springtime with pink tulips in bloom. Along the fence on stone shelves is a collection of Japanese asarums. Crepe myrtle

'Natchez' (*below, left*) is noted for its cinnamon-colored bark. Large leaf mondo grass (*Ophiopogon jaburan*) is in the foreground

beyond which are two examples of Farfugium japonicum with kidney-shaped leaves both green and variegated. In the summer, the rich

greens (*below, center*) are set off by a large pink flowered angel's wing begonia (*B. 'Sophie Cecile'*) backed by pink impatiens. To the left

is a topiary ring of maiden hair vine (*Muehlenbeckia complexa*) and caladium 'John Peel.' The neat arrangement of pots (*below, right*)

has a focal center where barrel hoops are used to support annual vines in the summer months. Here are the broad leaves of foxgloves

(*Digitalis purpurea Cvs.*), red leaf mustard (*Brassica juncea Var. foliosa*), and variegated thistle with rye grass in the forward pot. ❧

WHEN THE PROPERTY WAS PURCHASED IN 1976, THE LOFTY BACK YARD CONTAINED AN IMMENSE SUGAR HACKBERRY tree (*Celtis laevigata*), which was soon felled, and a lot of ivy. Excavation revealed evidence of an earlier garden that included slate tiles, which were incorporated into a new layout together with millstones (*right*). This verdant garden, which receives little sun, appears most tranquil when viewed from the balcony, which is ensconced in Clematis Armandii. Liriope is used as a ground cover, and the foliage includes evergreen podocarpus, fatsia, cast-iron plant (*Aspidistra elatior*), and perennial elephant ears (*Colocasia esculenta*). The pedestal (*below*) was found locally and is topped with an 1880's kerosene lamp. The lavabo came from Vienna. The stone bench was bought from a sale after a fire at a local estate and on it sits Rosie, a cavalier King Charles Spaniel and noted film star. ❧

THE OWNERS MOVED INTO THIS HOUSE IN 1979, SO BY LATER-DAY STANDARDS, IT IS ONE OF THE MORE MATURE gardens in the city. It is laid out with beds around a terrace (*below, right*) paved with tabby squares made from scallops that give a pinkish cast. To the left of the bench is a bright orange nasturtium. Farfugium japonicum, mature honeysuckle and chocolate soldier clover make a nice display. The hypertufa troughs are hand made by the gardener-owner. A trough (*below, left*) contains a woody azalea and club moss along with a rare species of miniature impatiens collected in Peru. Along the wall (*right*) is a white Cherokee Rose, the state flower of Georgia. This species of rose has become naturalized in the Southeast and makes a good garden plant with regular training and pruning. Between the river birch trees are the brilliant blooms of native honeysuckle (*following pages, top right*). Confederate jasmine (*Trachelospermum jasminoides*) is also known as Star jasmine (*following pages, bottom right*). Blooming in the spring is yesterday-today-and-tomorrow (*Brunfelsia australis*), named for the flowers that change color as they age (*following pages, top left*). The gloriosa lily (*G. Rothschildiana*) can be coaxed into bloom by altering the watering regimen (*following pages, bottom left*). ❧

IN 1987, THE BACK YARD OF THIS 1870 HOUSE WAS A DIRT FIELD WITH A MAGNOLIA TREE. The

architect/owner, together with a student, went through an extensive design process based on utopian principals and

relying on found objects to generate appropriate forms. Along the eastern brick wall covered with fig vine (*below, left; right*),

a black steel grating bridges over a fish pond and forms the path that leads from the house to the lane. The water

is brought back by way of a runnel and is carried to a deep reservoir where it is filtered and recirculated. An innovative

drip line is snaked along the top of the garden wall to irrigate the fig vine and narrow bed. The vegetable garden (*below, right*)

sits on top of a three-car garage that was constructed along the lane. ❧

HOW TO GARDEN WITH NO GARDEN! WITH INGENUITY AND AN INNATE SENSE OF DESIGN, THE OWNER

has tiered the narrow strip between the house and sidewalk (*below, right*) to hold a variety of pots of spring plants that

enjoy morning sun. The window box (*below, left*) seems to be thoroughly admired. ❧

Not many gardens in the historic district can boast a swimming pool. This one was installed when the house was renovated in 1975 (*below, left*) and is edged with urns holding pink geraniums and trailing ivy. The lower level of the house has well-tended fig vines on the wall, and to the right, a mature pittosporum hedge.

The sculpture by Ivan Bailey (*below, right*), commissioned in 1990, is alongside the carriage house, which may be older than the house proper. It represents a deep-sea wreck and is made up of various maritime objects. Bailey also designed and made the railings on the deck, which is terminated with a basin and lion's head fountain.

THIS LONG NARROW GARDEN RUNS PARALLEL TO THAT OF THE HUGH M. COMER HOUSE NEXT DOOR. It was designed by Eleanor Sasser early in the 1990s after the 1872 house had undergone a thorough renovation. Plantings include (*right, top*) Camellias, a dwarf Japanese maple (*Acer palmatum* 'Burgundy Lace') and Confederate jasmine. The lawn and plantings contrast nicely with the discipline of the brick paths and walls, which can be enjoyed when looked down upon from the verandah (*right, bottom*). This large, single white Camellia japonica (*below*) is featured in the garden. ❧

THE DANIEL ROBERTSON HOUSE *(built 1853)*

THIS DELIGHTFUL LITTLE GARDEN HAS A DIAMOND SHAPED BED (*below, right*) PLANTED WITH YELLOW snap dragons (*Antirrhinum*) set in paths of crushed sea shells and with supporting corner beds. On pleasant days, the owners can open their back gate and entertain guests (*below, left*). ❧

ARCHITECT J UAN C. B ERTTOTTO DESIGNED THIS CHARMING GARDEN IN THE 1970 S. C AST -IRON STEPS (*below, left*) descend from the parlor level to a brick patio surrounded by rich greenery including holly fern (*Cyrtomium falcatum*), strawberry begonia (*Saxifraga stolonifera*), and umbrella plant (*Cyperus alternifolius*). Ivy on the brick wall strikingly leaps over the inset lion's head. Fig vine creeps over the lace brick wall behind the pool (*below, right*). The delightful fountain is backed by cast-iron plants (*Aspidistra elatior*).

THERE WAS VIRTUALLY NOTHING HERE WHEN THE HOUSE WAS PURCHASED IN 1990 OTHER THAN A SMALL PYRACANTHA, which has since grown into a sturdy tree. The circulation problem was to deal with six points of access: from the street, the lane, the garage, the carriage house apartment, the garden apartment, and the upper deck, and there was a need to pull the whole space together.

Graham Landscape Architecture of Annapolis, Maryland, designed the garden including the redwood structures built by Steven Tannenberg. Two features are the Palmetto palm (*Sabal palmetto*), which was brought in from a nursery in Hilton Head (*below, left*), and the pond (*right*) with its bubbling fountain made from Georgia red granite. In pots there is 'Tropicana' Canna (*C. hybrid var. 'Phasion'*), angel wing begonia (*B. 'Torch'*), and a red passion flower vine (*Passiflora vitifolia*) climbing up a key lime tree (*citrus aurantifolia*). The planting has an evergreen bone structure with seasonal color in summer months when the sun reaches into the garden over the three-story house. Holly fern (*Cyrtomium falcatum*), an espaliered Parrotia persica, and Clematis armandii are some features (*below, right*). ❧

The Independent Presbyterian Church

WHEN THE AXSON MEMORIAL BUILDING WAS BUILT BEHIND THE CHURCH IN 1928 ON THE SITE OF THE MANSE, a courtyard was created leaving the western windows of the sanctuary unobstructed and making a clear definition between the two buildings. A pool with a wrought-iron fountain (*top, left*) is the centerpiece of this symmetrical layout. Red and white begonias make a fine show in the spring to be replaced by pansies in the winter months. ❧

The Augustus Barie House *(on Charlton Street)*

THE GARDEN FACES NORTH. SIDE GARDENS (*top, right*) WERE OFTEN DESIGNED TO BE ENJOYED FROM VERANDAHS. This one was revitalized in the early 1990s. The pool in the middle was set in a former parterre bed, but the freestanding wrought-iron gate was retained as an eye-catching folly. The origin of the leaden nymph is not known, but it was obtained to provide a focal point. Herbaceous borders line the lawn. ❧

The Thomas Holcombe House

LOUISA FARRAND WOOD DESIGNED THIS GARDEN FOR HERSELF IN THE EARLY 1980S. SINCE SHE AND HER husband spent their summers in Maine, the garden was intended to be fully enjoyed in fall, winter, and spring. Louisa Farrand Wood was the niece of Beatrix Farrand, America's first female landscape architect, and the great-niece of Edith Wharton. Her mother, Mrs. Livingston Farrand, designed the extensive gardens at Cornell University during her husband's presidency there. The current owners have maintained the garden in its original design (*below*). Azaleas abound. They are in the central beds with four boxwoods and a nice border of tightly knit ivy. Tea olives (*Osmanthus fragrans*) shade the south side of the house. ❧

BUILT IN 1820 BY ISAIAH DAVENPORT, A MASTER BUILDER FROM RHODE ISLAND, THIS HOUSE WAS SAVED FROM THE wrecking ball in 1955, which lead to the formation of the Historic Savannah Foundation. The Foundation now owns the house. It was opened to the public in 1963, but the garden was not created until 1976 as a bicentennial project of the Trustees Garden Club. After some years of neglect, largely through lack of funds, restoration work is now under way. The terra-cotta urn (*below*) is planted with white snapdragon and petunias surrounded by fledgling Japanese holly. Beyond is a dogwood tree and crepe myrtle. A burgeoning knot-garden (*right*) has rosemary, sage, chard, baby lettuce, and other herbs. Spring planting in the circular bed (*following pages*) includes snap dragon (*Antirrhinum*), pansies, and Johnny jump ups (*viola hybrida*) with roses in the central urn. ❧

AN INTRIGUING COMPLEX OF SPACES GIVES AN ATMOSPHERE SURPRISINGLY REDOLENT OF TUSCANY OR PROVENCE. Approached through a courtyard (*below*) that also gives access to apartments, an arched entry in a lace brick wall is flanked by pittosporum and a pair of clay pots that have a design based on cotton baskets. Through the wrought-iron gate is what may be called an outdoor living room. In one of the areas adjacent to the garden is a sculpted monkey (*right*) — an amusing family symbol — set amid holly fern (*Cyrtomium falcatum*) and Anise (*Illicium sp.*). In front of the wall (*following pages*) covered with Confederate jasmine (*Trachelospermum jasminoides*) is a bed of old-fashioned purple Persian shield (*Strobilanthus dyeranus*) and caladium 'Miss Muffet.' At either end are 60-year-old tea olives (*Osmanthus fragrans*). The street lamp came from Charleston, South Carolina.

The Charles V. Hutchins House

AN ESTABLISHED (ALBEIT SOMEWHAT OVERGROWN) SIDE GARDEN HERE WAS DESTROYED DURING THE YEARLONG renovation of the house in 1992. It was decided to lower the level of the ground and form a series of scallops with low brick retaining walls supporting flower beds around the sides. A new small pool with the existing fountain (*below*) creates a central feature. Under the direction of John McEllen, a completely new planting was undertaken. Not only can the owners enjoy seeing this from above, but lucky passersby can inspect it through the wrought-iron fencing along the street. Through an old latticed wooden archway laden with confederate jasmine, there is a bower with a crazy paving path leading past a clump of canna lily (*c. 'Bengal'*) to a pond backed by healthy bamboo (*right*). By the foot of the steps from the balcony (*following pages*) are petunias and pink mandevilla and opposite is an array of lavender flowered agapanthus and purple salvia backed by a European Fan Palm (*Chamaerops humilis*).

SPRINGTIME ON THE BALCONY OUTSIDE THE KITCHEN PRESENTS A TRULY **G**ALLIC AIR. WITH A

background of hedra ivy and Boston ferns overhead (*below*), color is provided by pots of geraniums and petunias. The

table is set with an Italian ceramic 'artichoke' tureen and souvenirs of France. A highly prized feature is a 4-foot-deep

pool (*right*) containing a 20-year-old collection of Japanese fish, primarily Koi, which seem to belie their name before

the camera. Stairs with Confederate jasmine lead down to the brick courtyard (*following pages*) where a raised bed

sports an array of herbs including rosemary growing in an olive oil jar brought from Provence. ❧

The owner of this house became fascinated with bonsai after receiving one as a gift. Recognizing that this was an ideal pursuit for a grower with a small garden, the owner created a beautiful bonsai garden. The rectangular Koi pond was added to the center of the courtyard, which had been designed by Clermont H. Lee in the late 1960s, making useful narrow beds at its perimeter. The garden (*below, left*) is intended to accommodate and demonstrate seasonal differences with staples that flourish year-round, such as the variegated sedge grass (*Carex morrowsii 'Aureo-variegata'*) at the corners of the pond and the Horse Tail (*Equisetum hyemale*) in it. Pansies bloom in the spring in pots in front of dwarf heavenly bamboo (*Nandina domestica 'Nana Purpurea'*). The bronze cranes are a recent acquisition. Fallen leaves (*below, right*) from the 30-year-old Gingko tree spell autumn. The sugar hackberry bonsai (*Celtis laevigata*) in the blue glazed tray (*right*) shows its main root. Little white mud figures are considered appropriate since they, too, are dwarfs. The two della Robbia-like wall plaques came from Italy. In early summer there is a blaze of color (*following pages*), including a robust hydrangea, geraniums, petunias, and yellow Straw Flower (*Helichrysum bracteatum*) on a white circular table. The bonsai shelf was designed by the owner, set at a comfortable height for working. ❧

THE HOUSE WAS DESIGNED BY WILLIAM JAY IN 1818, BUT THERE IS NO RECORD OF A GARDEN PLAN. THE PROPERTY was acquired by the Historic Savannah Foundation in the late 1960s, and a garden was laid out by the Trustees Garden Club in the 1970s. The garden pavilion was dedicated to Mary Dusenburg Tiedeman in 1984. Now owned by the Ships of the Sea Maritime Museum, the grounds have been extended by the closing of a small adjacent street, creating the largest garden in the Landmark District. A planting design by John McEllen has enhanced the Trustees Garden Club design, using native plants or those available in Savannah before 1820. With azaleas in the foreground (*below*), two spectacular topiary azaleas in pots watch over a white classical 'temple' — formally an official 19th-century U.S. Government weather station that had once stood in Wright Square. Behind the pot of glorious verbena 'Homestead Purple' and emerging canna lilies (*c. 'Bengal'*) there is a splendid carved Italian limestone urn (*right*), one of a pair carved in Italy for an English estate, early in the 20th century.

Through trunks of Foster's Holly trees (*Ilex fosteri*) that were planted by the Trustees Garden Club (*pages 100–101*) are dwarf Yaupon hollies with the pavillion in the background. Color is provided beyond by snapdragons (*Antirrhinum*) and angel's trumpet (*Brugmansia cv.*). A large terra-cotta pot tucked into a dwarf yaupon holly hedge (*page 102*) holds Icelandic poppies (*Papaver nudicaule*), viola, and sweet alyssum (*Lobularia maritima*) with giant red mustard (*Brassica sp.*). The pond and fountain (*page 103*) were donated in the 1980s by Dr. and Mrs. Robert Logan in memory of their young son, Robert. In front of canna lilies (*c. 'Bengal'*) are purple oxalis, violas, and pink Verbena (*left*). The elegant wire topiary urn from a Long Island, New York, estate (*below, left*) contains 'Torch' angel wing begonias with fig vine at its base. A fig-vine-smothered wall is adjacent to a hedge of Yaupon holly (*below, right*). Azaleas, verbena (*Cv. Homestead Purple*), and Yeddo Hawthorne (*Rhaphiolepis umsellata 'Majestic Beauty'*) bloom in front of Foster's Holly (*Ilex x attenuata 'Foster's #2'*) with the beautifully restored Scarbrough house beyond (*following pages*). ❧

SQUARES ARE THE ESSENCE OF THE CITY. OF VARYING DIMENSIONS AND LANDSCAPING, THEY ARE THE SPACES AROUND which the citizens work and live. Wright and Telfair (formally St. James) are two of the original four squares laid out by James Oglethorpe in 1733. All squares on Bull Street have monuments in them today: In Wright, it was placed in 1833 for William Washington Gordon, founder and president of the Central of Georgia Railway. The old Telfair House, now the museum of art, can be seen across the daffodils. Reynolds and Washington (1734) squares demonstrate the way in which downtown pedestrian traffic can flow through them, and benches afford the opportunity for rest and conversation. Columbia (1799) was redesigned by the Trustees Garden Club in the 1970s, creating the central pond with a fountain brought in from Wormsloe plantation, the house of Noble Jones, a distinguished first colonist. The Kehoe House, festooned with fig vine (*Ficus radicans*) and confederate jasmine,

*T*he Old Telfair House

*W*ashington Square

Wright Square

Kehoe House on Columbia Square

can be seen through the azaleas. There is a fountain in Orleans (1815), a square that was spatially altered by the destruction

of the buildings on its western side in 1968 to make way for the Civic Center. Madison (1837) and Crawford (1841) squares

illustrate a contrast in usage. In the former, dominated by the monument to Sgt. Jasper, who fell in the siege of Savannah in 1779,

dinner is to be served for a function sponsored by the Savannah College of Art and Design. In the latter, there is a playground.

Troup, with an armillary sphere in the middle, and Whitefield, with its gazebo frequently used for weddings, are among the last

squares to be formed in 1851. When the main streets were laid out, they were 75 feet wide. When it came to paving them, spaces

were created between the roads and sidewalks called 'tree lawns.' In these areas, the city provides trees, and the householders

are free to plant. Oleander is very popular, set against some of the decorative ironwork for which the city is noted. The iron railing

of the E.M. Schroeder House is in fact a copy of one seen near the harbor in Baltimore, Maryland. With geraniums added, it

makes a most public spirited gesture together with the Asiatic jasmine cascading from a window box. On Tattnall Street, Chinese

wisteria with ivy makes a typical combination. Lantana is ubiquitous in the squares. A fountain and trees with Spanish moss are

found in Forsyth Park. A good deal of the character of Savannah is created by its trees — magnolias, live oaks, crepe myrtle,

and palmetto palms, all livened by suspending gray streams of native Spanish moss (*Tillandsia usneoides*). Not a true moss,

Reynolds Square

Orleans Square

***M**adison Square*

***T**roup Square*

***C**rawford Square*

Whitefield Square

Lantana

Oleander

Wisteria

Tattnall Street

E.M. Schroeder House

Colonial Park Cemetery

Tree Lawn

Pei Ling Garden of the Arts

Jones Street

The Waving Girl

Spanish moss is actually the northernmost example of the Bromeliaceae, related to the pineapple. Although it is not a parasite, it sometimes can thrive to the point of smothering its host, particularly deciduous trees like the crepe myrtle and dogwood. The Fragrant Garden for the Blind, the first of its kind in the Southeast, was the imaginative project of Savannah garden clubs. It was dedicated in 1963. To celebrate the 20th anniversary of the Savannah College of Art and Design, a competition was sponsored for the design of Functional Follies. Out of 116 entries, 20 were awarded commissions. "Be It Ever So Humble" by Patrick Dougherty was erected in Forsyth Park. The college built the Pei Ling Garden of the Arts, which represents international influences, including African-American, Asian, English, and French sections. The statue of the Waving Girl (Florence Martus, who greeted ships between 1887 and 1931) was sculpted by Felix de Weldon. It stands in Morrell Park. Beyond is the Olympic Flame monument by Ivan Bailey. ❧

Functional Folly in Forsyth Park

The Fragrant Garden for the Blind

*T*he following list is an attempt to identify, by both botanical and common name, many plants that have proved successful in the area of Historic Savannah.
*Those featured in this book.

Botanical Name	Common Name	Origin
Abelia floribunda	Mexican Abelia	Mexico
Acer japonicum	Full-moon Maple	Japan
*Acer palmatum 'Burgundy Lace'	Lace Leaf Japanese Maple	Japan
Acer saccharum	Sugar maple (white)	Japan/USA
*Achillea sp.	Yarrow	N. Hemisphere
*Agapanthus africanus	Lily of the Nile	Africa
*Agave americana	Century plant	Mexico
Ajuga reptans	Carpet Bugle	Europe
*Albisia julibrissin	Mimosa	E. Asia
*Antirrhinum majus	Snapdragon	Mediterranean
Arctotis stoechadifolia	African Daisy	S. Africa
Ardisia crenata 'coral berry'	Ardisia	Asia
*Ardisia japonica	Marlberry	Asia
*Arundinaria	Bamboo	Tropics/Subtropics
*Arundinaria gigantea	Canebreak	S.E. USA
*Asarum sp.	Wild Ginger	Asia/USA/Europe
*Asparagus densi florus 'myers'	Foxtail Fern	S. Africa
*Asparagus setaceus	Lace Fern	S. Africa
Asparagus densiflorus 'Sprengeri'	Asparagus Fern	S. Africa
*Aspidistra elatior	Cast Iron Plant	Japan
*Astilbe x hybrida	Astilbe	S.E. Asia/N. Amer.
Aucuba japonica	Japanese Laurel	Japan
Azalea, see Rhododendron		
*Azolla caroliniana	Fairy Moss	S.E. USA
Basella alba 'Rubra'	Malabar Spinach	Tropical Africa/Asia
*Begonia sp.	many	Trop & Sub Trop
*Begonia B. 'Torch'	Torch Begonia	Sub-tropics
Belamcanda chinensis	Blackberry Lily	China/Japan
*Berberis julianae	Barberry	China
*Betula nigra	River Birch	E. USA
*Brassica juncea var. foliosa	Giant Red Mustart	Japan
*Brugmansia x candida	Angel's Trumpet	S. America
*Brunfelsia australis	Yesterday-Today-and-Tomorrow	Brazil

Botanical Name	Common Name	Origin
Buxus microphylla var. japonica	Japanese Boxwood	Japan
Buxus microphylla var. koreana	Korean Boxwood	Korea
Buxus sempervirens	Common Boxwood	Europe & W. Asia
Caladium x hortulanum	Fancy Leaf Caladium	Tropical S. America
Camellia japonica	Camellia	Japan/Korea
Camellia Sasanqua	Sasanqua	Japan
Campsis radicans	Trumpet Vine	USA
Canna hybrida/Var. Phasion	Tropicana	Garden Origin
Canna indica	Red Canna	Central America
Canna Cv. 'Bengal'	Bengal Tiger Canna Lily	Garden Origin
Carex morrowii 'Aurea-variegata'	Sedge	Japan
Carya glabra	Pignut Hickory	E. USA
Carya illinoinensis	Pecan	E. USA
Cassia bicapsularis	Cassia	Egypt/India
Catharantus roseus	Vinca	Madagascar
Celtis laevigata	Sugar Hackberry	Tropical N. Hemis.
Cephalotaxus harringtonia 'Fastigata'	Plum Yew	Japan
Cercis canadensis	Eastern Redbud	E. USA
Chaenomeles japonica	Japanese Quince	Japan
Chamaecyparis lawsoniana	Oregon Cedar	USA
Chamaerops humilis	European Fan Palm	Mediterranean
Chrysanthemum leucanthemum	Ox-eye Daisy	Europe/Asia
Chrysanthemum x morifolium	Chrysanthemum	China
Citrus aurantiifolia	Key Lime	India
Clematis Armandii	Evergreen Clematis	Central & W. China
Clematis virginiana	Virgin's Bower	S.E. USA
Clethra alnifolia	White Alder; Sweet Pepperbush	E. USA
Coleus x hybridus	Coleus	Java, or hybrid
Colocasia esculenta	Elephant's Ear	Java
Consolida ambigua	Larkspur	Mediterranean
Cornus florida	Dogwood	E. USA
Cortaderia selloana	Pampas Grass	S. America
Crinum americanum	Southern Swamp Crinum	S.E. USA
Cupressus sempervirens	Italian Cypress	E. Europe/W. Asia
Cycas revoluta	Sago Palm	S. Japan
Cyperus alternifolius	Umbrella Grass	Madagascar
Cyrtomium falcatum	Holly Fern	Japan/India
Daphne odora	February Daphne	China/Japan
Delphinium sp.	Delphinium or Larkspur	N. Temp. Zone
Dianthus plumarius Var. albiflorus	White grass pink	Carpathians

Botanical Name	Common Name	Origin
*Digitalis purpurea cvs.	Foxglove	Portugal/Spain
*Eichhornia crassipes	Water hyacinth	Brazil
*Elaeagnus angustifolia	Russian Olive	Europe/W. Asia
Endymion hispanicus	Spanish squill	Portugal/Spain
*Equisetum hyemale	Horsetail	USA
Eriobotrya japonica	Loquat	Cent. China/S. Japan
Erythrina herbacea	Cardinal-spear/Cherokee Bean	S.E. USA/Mexico
Euonymus japonica	Japanese Euonymus	Japan
*Farfugium japonica	Ligularia	Japan
X Fatshedera lizei	Tree Ivy	France
*Fatsia japonica	Japanese Aralia	Japan
Ficus carica	Common Fig	Mediterranean
*Ficus pumila	Fig Vine	E. Asia/China
Fortunella margarita	Kumquat	S. China
Franklinia alatamaha	Franklin Tree	Georgia
Galega officinalis	Goats Rue	Europe/Asia
*Gardenia jasminoides	Cape Jasmine	China/Japan
*Gaura lindheimeri	Guara	N. America
Geranium maculatum	Wild Geranium	E. USA
Gerbera Jamesoni	Transvaal Daisy	S. Africa
*Ginko biloba	Maidenhair Tree	China
*Gloriosa Rothschildiana	Gloriosa Lily	Africa/India
*Hedera helix cvs.	Ivy	Europe
*Hedychium coronarium	Butterfly Ginger	India
*Helichrysum bracteatum	Straw Flower	Australia
Hibiscus Rosa-sinensis	Hawaiian Hibiscus	Tropical Asia
Hibiscus trionum	Flower-of-an-hour	Central Africa
Hosta plantaginea	Hosta; Plantain-lily	China/Japan
Hyacinthus orientalis, var.	Roman Hyacinth	Mediterranean
*Hydrangea macrophylla	Big Leaf Hydrangea	Japan
Hymenocallis caroliniana	Spider Lily	S.E. USA
Ilex Aquifolium	English Holly	Europe
*Ilex x attenuata 'Foster #2'	Foster's Holly	USA
Ilex cassine	Dahoon	S.E. USA
Ilex 'Savannah' x attenuata	Savannah Holly	USA
*Ilex vomitoria 'Nana'	Swarf Yaupon Holly	USA
*Ilex vomitoria 'Shelling's Dwarf'	Shelling's Holly	USA
*Illicium sp.	Anise	S.E. Asia/S.E. USA
Impatiens wallerana	Impatiens; Patient Lucy	E. Africa
Iris germanica	Flag; Bearded Iris	Europe

Botanical Name	Common Name	Origin
*Juniperus chinensis Var. 'torulosa'	Chinese Juniper	E. Asia
Juniperus horizontalis 'Wiltonii'	Blue Rug Juniper	North America
Justicia brandegeana	Shrimp plant	Mexico
Juniperus torulosa	Hollywood Juniper	USA
*Lagerstroemia indica	Crape Myrtle	China/Korea
*Lantana camara cvs.	Lantana	Tropical S. America
Lavandula angustifolia	English Lavender	Mediterranean
Leucojum aestivum	Summer Snowflake	Europe
Leucojum vernum	Spring Snowflake	Central Europe
Leucothoe fontanesiana	Dog Hobble	S.E. USA
Ligustrum ovalifolium	Ligustrum; Privet	Japan
Ligustrum vulgare	Common Privet	Europe/N. Africa
Lilium longiflorum var. eximum	Easter Lily	Japan
*Limonium sp.	Statice	Coastal Eur/N. Amer./Asia
Lindera obtusiloba	Pomegranate	S.E. Europe/S. Asia
*Liriope muscari	Lilyturf	Japan/China
Lobelia erinus	Edging Lobelia	S. Africa
*Lobularia maritima	Sweet Alyssum	Europe
Lonicera japonica	Japanese Honeysuckle	China/Japan
*Lonicera sempervirens	Native Trumpet Honeysuckle	E. USA
Lycoris radiata	Spider Lily	China/Japan
Macfadyena unguis-cati	Catsclaw; Funnelcreeper	Central America
*Magnolia grandiflora	Southern Magnolia	S.E. USA
Mahonia aquifolium	Holly Grape	N.W. North America
Mahonia nervosa	Oregon Grape	N.W. USA
Malus pumila	Callaway Garden Crab Apple	USA
*Mandevilla x amabilis	Mandevilla	Mexico to Argentina
Melia azedarach	Chinaberry	Asia
Michelia Figo	Banana Shrub	China
Mirabilis jalapa	Four O'Clock	Tropical America
*Muehlenbeckia complexa	Maidenhair Vine	New Zealand
Musa x paradisiaca	Banana	Tropics
*Nandina domestica Nana Purpurea	Heavenly Bamboo	China/Japan
*Narcissus hybrida	Daffodil	Cen. Europe to Japan
*Nephrolepis exaltata cv. 'Bostoniensis'	Boston Fern	Florida to Brazil/E. Africa
*Nephrolepis cordifolia	Fishbone Fern	Florida to Brazil/E. Africa
*Nerium Oleander	Oleander	Mediterranean/Japan
Ocium basilicum	Basil	Tropical Old World
Oenothera biennis	Evening Primrose	E. USA
*Ophiopogon jaburan	Big leaf mondo Grass	Japan

Botanical Name	Common Name	Origin
*Ophiopogon japonicus 'Nana'	Dwarf Mondo Grass	Japan/Korea
*Osmanthus fragrans	Tea Olive	E. Asia/China
*Oxalis sp.	Shamrock	S. Africa/S.E. USA
Palm Chrysalidacarpus	Areca Palm	USA
*Papaver nudicaule	Icelandic Poppy	Arctic Regions E./W. Hemis.
Parkinsonia aculeata	Jerusalem Thorn	Tropical America
*Parrotia persica	Persian Ironwood	N. Persia
Parthenocissus quinquefolia	Virginia Creeper	N. America
*Passiflora vitifolia	Red Passion Vine	Brazil
*Pelargonium x domesticum	Geranium	S. Africa
*Petunia x hybrida cvs.	Petunia	Argentina
Philadelphus coronarius	Mock Orange	Europe
Phlox bifida	White Phlox	E. USA
Photinia glabra	Japanese Photinia	Japan
Pimpinella anisum	Anise	Eurasia/Africa
Pinus echniata	Shortleaf Pine	S.E. USA
*Pinus parviflora	Japanese White Pine	Japan
*Pistia stratiotes	Water lettuce	S.E. USA - Tropical
*Pittosporum Tobira	Japanese Mock Orange	China, Japan
Plumbago auriculata	Cape Leadwort	S. Africa
*Podocarpus macrophyllus	Japanese Yew	Japan
Portulaca grandiflora	Portulaca; Rose Moss	S. America
Prunus Mume	Flowering Apricot	China
Prunus caroliniana	Cherry Laurel	S.E. USA
Prunus persica	Peach	China
*Pyracantha coccinea	Fire Thorn	Asia Minor
Quercus acuta	Japanese Evergreen Oak	Japan
Quercus nigra	Water Oak	S.E. USA
*Quercus virginiana	Live Oak	S.E. USA
Raphiolepis indica	Indian Hawthorn	S. China
*Raphiolepis umbellata 'Majestic Beauty'	Yedda Hawthorn	S. japan
Rhododendron cv.	Ghent hybrid Azalea	Belgian hybrid
Rhododendron cv.	Waka-bisu Azalea	Japanese hybrid
*Rhododendron hybrida	Azalea	Japanese hybrid
Rhododendron obtusum	Kirishima Azalea	Japan
Rhododendron Simsii	Indian Azalea	China
Robinia Elliottii	Rose Acacia	S.E. USA
*Rosa banksiae	Banksia Rose	China
*Rosa laevigata	Cherokee Rose	China
Rosa mutabilis	China Rose	China

Botanical Name	Common Name	Origin
Rosa cv.	Houston Tree Rose	USA hybrid
Rosa cv.	Savannah Tree Rose	USA hybrid
*Rosmarinus officinalis	Rosemary	Mediterranean
Rudbeckia hirta	Black-eyed Susan	USA
Russelia equistiformis Cv. 'setiformis'	Firecracker Plant	Mexico/S. America
*Sabal Palmetto	Cabbage Palm	S.E. USA/Mexico
*Salvia 'Indigo Spires'	Indigo Spires Salvia	Temp. regions E & W Hemis.
Salvia officinalis	Garden Sage	Mediterranean
Sapium sebiferum	Chinese Tallow Tree	China/Japan
*Saxifraga stolonifera	Strawberry Begonia	China/Japan
*Selaginella Kraussiana	Club Moss	Africa, Madeira
Smilax lanceolata	Jackson Brier-Smilax	Georgia-Panama
Spiraea x bumalda	Spirea	hybrid
Stokesia laevis	Stokesia; Stokes Aster	S.E. USA
Strelitzia reginae	Bird of Paradise	S. Africa
*Strobilanthes Dyerianus	Persian Shield	Burma
Tagetes patula	French marigold	Mexico/Guatemala
*Tillandsia usneoides	Spanish moss	S.E. USA
Torenia fournieri	Torenia; Bluewings	Tropical Asia/Africa
*Trachelospermum jasminoides	Confederate Jasmine	China
Trachelospermum asiaticum	Asian Jasmine	Japan
*Trifolium pratense 'Chocolate Soldier'	Chocolate Soldier Clover	Europe
*Tropaeolum majus	Nasturtium	Peru, Columbia, Brazil
Tulbaghia violacea	Society Garlic	S. Africa
*Tulipa hybrida	Tulip	Siberia, Turkey, China, Japan
Verbascum phlomoides	Mullein	S. Europe
*Verbena canadensis 'Homestead Purple'	Homestead purple Verbena	S. USA
Verbena laciniata	Moss Verbena	S. America
Viburnum odoratissimum	Sweet Viburnum	Japan/Formosa
Vinca minor	Periwinkle	Europe
Viola odorata	Sweet Violet	Europe
*Viola tricolor	Johnny Jump Up	E. USA
*Viola x wittrockiana cvs.	Pansy	E. USA
Vitex agnus-castus	Chaste Tree	E. Europe
Vitis rotundifolia	Muscadine Grape; Scuppernong	N. America
Weigela Cv. Candida	Weigela	N. China hybrid
*Wisteria sinensis	Chinese Wisteria	China
Yucca gloriosa	Spanish-bayonet	S.E. USA
Zamia floridana	Zamia; Coontie	Florida
*Zephyranthes grandiflora	Rain Lily	S. Mexico to Guatemala

THANK YOU

This book would not have been possible without the kindness, generosity, expertise, and commitment of many people. Historic Savannah Foundation is deeply grateful for their cooperation.

Mr. & Mrs. Leopold Adler II
Anne-Marie Andrews
Hall of Apothecaries Library, London
Mr. & Mrs. Park Callahan
Porter Carswell
Mr. & Mrs. Dale Critz, Jr.
Isaiah Davenport House
Sally Davis
Mr. & Mrs. H. Clark Deriso
Dr. & Mrs. Edward F. Downing
Mr. & Mrs. John Duncan
Jeff Fulton
The Garden Club of Georgia, Inc.
Dr. Don Gardner
Georgia Historical Society
Mr. & Mrs. Karl Graham
Green-Meldrim House
Dr. & Mrs. Dieter Gunkle
Mr. & Mrs. Walter C. Hartridge
Mr. & Mrs. William Hahn
Mr. & Mrs. Edward Hill
Independent Presbyterian Church
Emory Jarrott
John F. Johnson
Mills B. Lane IV
Clermont Lee
Andrew Low House

Juliette Gordon Low House
James Maury
John McEllen
Mr. & Mrs. Richard Middleton
James W. Morton III
Dr. Frederick Meyer
Mr. & Mrs. Richard H. Meyer
Savannah Park and Tree Commission
Mr. & Mrs. Greg Parker
Allen P. Paterson
Mr. & Mrs. Richard Platt
Mr. & Mrs. B.J. Poole
Elizabeth Reiter
Mrs. Juan Carlo Rossini
St. John's Episcopal Church
Savannah College of Art and Design
Sharon L. Saseen
Ships of the Sea Maritime Museum
Daniel Snyder
Mr. & Mrs. William W. Sprague, Jr.
Albert H. Stoddard
Mrs. Huguenin Thomas, Jr.
Richardson, Owens-Thomas House
Nancy Tobin
Trustees Garden Club
Mr. & Mrs. Joseph A. Webster

SOURCES

Bailey, L.H. & E.Z. (compiled by): *Hortus Third*: Macmillan Publishing Company, New York: 1976

Conran, John: *The American Landscape*: Oxford University Press: New York: 1973

ed. Coulter, E. Merton: *The Journal of Peter Gordon, 1732-35*: University of Georgia Press, Athens: 1963

D'Alonzo, Mary Beth: *Street Cars of Chatham County*: Arcadia Publishing: Charleston, S.C. 1999

ed. Harper, Francis: *The Travels of William Bartram*: The University of Georgia Press: Athens & London: 1998

Hobhouse, Penelope: *Plants in Garden History*: Pairlion Books Limited: London, 1992

ed. Huxley, Anthony: *The New Royal Horticultural Society Dictionary of Gardening*: Grove's Dictionaries Inc., New York, 1999

ed. Inscoe, John C.: *James Edward Oglethorpe*: The Georgia Historical Society: Savannah, Georgia: 1997

ed. Jackson, Harvey H. and Spalding, Phinizy: *Forty Years of Diversity. Essays on Colonial Georgia*: The University of Georgia Press: Athens: 1984

Leighton, Ann: *American Gardens in the Eighteenth Century*: Houghton Mifflin Company: Boston: 1976

ed. Lockwood, Alice G. B.: *Gardens of Colony and State*: Charles Scribner's Sons: Vol. 1. 1931: Vol. 2. 1934

ed. Maccubbin, Robert P. and Martin, Peter: *British and American Gardens in the Eighteenth Century*: The Colonial Williamsburg Foundation, Williamsburg, Virginia: 1984

Mackay, Robert: *The Letters of Robert Macay to his Wife*: The University of Georgia Press: 1949 (compiled by Walter Hartridge)

ed. Marranca, Bennies: *American Garden Writing*: Penquin Books: 1988

Owens, Hubert B.: *Georgia's Planting Prelate*: University of Georgia Press, Athens: 1945

ed. Rainwater, Hattie C.: *Garden History of Georgia, 1733-1933*: The Peachtree Garden Club: Atlanta, Georgia: 1933

Ruse, Trevor, R. (introduced by): *The Most Delightful Country of the Universe*: The Beehive Press: Savannah, Georgia: 1972

Slosson, Elvenia (compiled by): *Pioneer American Gardening*: Coward-McCann Inc.: New York: 1951

Squibb, Robert: *The Gardeners Calendar*: Brown Thrasher Books: The University of Georgia Press, Athens: 1980

Wood, Louisa Farrand: Ray Ellis (illustrated by): *Behind Those Garden Walls in Historic Savannah*: 1982

End Paper: landscape drawings by Louise Yancey